TABLE OF CONTEN

Workbook Answers

Reading: Literature & Foundational Skills

The Alligator and the Squirrel answers

1. c
2. It was astonishing because it was very dangerous -- the alligator was very likely to catch the squirrel and eat him.
3. c
4. d
5. He let the squirrel go as a reward for making him laugh when he suggested that a tiny squirrel could help a mighty alligator
6. b
7. ne glect ed
8. a
9. b
10. a

Audrey's Braces answers

1. She thinks they will make her ugly and that other kids will ridicule her and won't want to be her friend.
2. four
3. c
4. Trojans
5. Audrey
6. Audrey's dad
7. d
8. (answers will vary) she was so happy that her friends
 still liked her and she wasn't going to be an outcast that she forgot about the little bit of physical pain she had.
9. e ven tu al ly
10. a

The Big Cupcake Heist answers

1. c
2. The word *heist* usually means a robbery of something very valuable, and the word *great* implies a big event, too, but since we're also told that it's all about a cupcake, we know the author is being humorous.
3. b
4. She is being **sarcastic**, which means she is saying the opposite of what she really means.
5. perfect pumpkin pastries
6. b
7. You would stress them more than the rest of the words.
8. c
9. a real mystery
10. Probably because she knew who ate the cupcake
11. He was making a joke about Jack being dressed like a pirate and Jaci being dressed like a nurse.

Anna Beth's Birthday Party answers

1. d
2. b
3. Because she knew it was Anna Beth's dad at the door
4. accomplish – it means to do, achieve, make happen, etc.
5. answers will vary

Josh's Big Game answers

1. ant i ci pa tion
2. c
3. d
4. a
5. d
6. un der es ti mat ed
7. c

8. it means they looked at each other at the same time
9. (answers will vary) they were concerned because Josh wanted to get back into the game and they wanted to make sure that didn't happen | they were each waiting for the other to speak | they knew how disappointed Josh was and wanted to choose their words carefully |
10. c
11. the fact that it was the conference championship game
12. d
13. Yes, because he can't wait 'til next year.
14. Dr. Huff
15. b

Meagan's Trip answers

1. The first meaning refers to the trip Meagan is taking to go hiking on Mount Ellis. The second meaning refers to her tripping over the root and breaking her arm.
2. Happy Valley Humane Society
3. animal doctor
4. vet er i nar i an
5. b
6. dry runs
7. a
8. c
9. She fell and broke her arm because she was running so fast she didn't notice the root and tripped over it. She was running in order to catch up to the others because she had stayed behind to take a photo.
10. preventing
11. (several possible answers)
each takes place during an outdoor athletic event (football game, hike)
main character suffers serious injury
characters are mainly young people
each involves a group of friends (football team, Girl Scout troop)
a long awaited day doesn't turn out the way the person had hoped it would

the main character is sad at first after being injured, but later cheers up thanks to friends

the main characters find out how much their friends care about them

12. The difference was that they were playing in a conference game, for the season championship. They couldn't quit playing, or they would have lost the game, and the championship. The best way to show Josh how much they cared for him was to keep playing and win the game. In the other story, the girls can come back to Mount Ellis and hike any time they want to.

A Boy and His Best Friend answers

1. (any two)
Travis calls his parents Ma and Pa
Ma drives a wagon, not a car
Travis attends a one-room school house
2. She means he has to do them every day and not get behind on them.
3. c
4. showering him with soft, wet kisses
5. Chance was Travis's shadow
6. b

Zeus vs. Typhon answers

1. the phrase *fate was with me that day* means that Zeus won the drawing to become ruler of the gods
2. b
3. dis guise
4. c
5. a
6. (any three) hurling thunderbolts, flying through the sky on winged horses, flames shooting out of the mouth of Typhon, 200 knives in Typhon's mouth, instant reattachment of toes and fingers, picking up a mountain and throwing it on Typhon, etc.
7. she is the goddess of wisdom
8. Tartarus

9. momentarily
10. a

Jack's First Christmas in Africa answers

1. He had to get used to eating strange food, and living in a hut
2. a maze ment
3. she meant she didn't really believe him when he said he was fine
4. He said *"fine, I guess"*, which doesn't sound like he means it, and he sighed
5. c

The Big 6th Grade Election answers

1. tallied
2. c
3. throw in the towel
4. to give up; to quit
5. answers will vary

Reading: Informational Texts

Gabby Douglas: Star of the Olympics answers

1. The Olympics
2. c
3. Opinion. That the Olympics take place every four years is a fact, but whether or not it's the most prestigious sports event is a matter of personal opinion. Millions of people would agree that the Olympics competition is the most prestigious sporting event in the world, but it is still an opinion, not a fact.
4. contagious
5. a family who allows someone from out of town to stay with them for an extended period of time
6. endorsement deals
7. ten
8. maneuver
9. c
10. d

Gabby Douglas: My Story answers

1. She would probably say no, because it was seeing her big sister doing gymnastics that led her to start training at such a young age.
2. Liang Chow
3. (answers will vary; here are some possible answers)
Gymnastics training is very hard
Training several hours a day is not only hard, but very boring
She missed her real family and old friends
She was injured or sick
She didn't think she was good enough to become a champion
4. This one. The other article is more focused on the Olympics and Gabby's previous accomplishments in gymnastics, but this article gives us more insight into what kind of person she is and the background she came from.
5. a

The Wonderful World of World Records answers

1. athletics
2. new records are set every year, so the book needs to updated with the new information
3. b
4. answers will vary
5. a

All About New Zealand answers

1. Lake Taupo
2. c
3. No. It is in the Southern Hemisphere, near the South Pole. America is a very long distance from New Zealand, in the Northern Hemisphere.
4. Hawaii
5. b

Earthquakes and Volcanoes in New Zealand answers

1. Answers will vary
2. 2006
3. February 3, 1931
4. 20 km
5. The previous article was written to encourage people to visit New Zealand. People tend to be scared of earthquakes, so if they knew that New Zealand has a lot of little earthquakes they might decide not to visit.

Metamorphosis answers

1. one
2. No
3. b
4. the leaves they're born on ("leaves" is also acceptable)
5. no

6. pupa

7 chrys a lis

8. Monarch

9. b

10. fas ci nat ing

11. cocoon

12. No; the baby may get around differently, but it has not changed into something completely different looking.

How to Make Spaghetti answers

1. not necessary; not required

2. following a good recipe

3. a

4. a bowl with holes in it for draining liquids from foods

5. it does not say how many servings the recipe provides

Weather Can Be Dangerous answers

1. c

2. take part | take part | engage

3. b

4. A blizzard features extreme cold and strong winds, in addition to snow.

5. c

Roger Staubach: Football Legend answers

1. d

2. c

3. con sec u tive

4. Most Valuable Player

5. to fulfill his obligation to serve in the Navy

6. the Heisman Trophy

7. d

8. answers will vary

No Ordinary House Cats! answers

1. intriguing
2. exotic
3. cheetahs; the article says they can outrun any animal over short distances
4. the jaguar; the article says no other animal can compete with its power
5. No
6. in trigu ing
7. re tract a ble
8. dies because it can't breath
9. the context is talking about the cheetah getting food by grabbing an animal around its throat
10. to inform--the article has elements of both entertainment and information, but its main purpose is to inform

Language

It's All Relative answers

1. Whoever
2. where
3. whom
4. when
5. who or that
6. which
7. Whichever
8. how
9. whose
10. that
11. where
12. which
13. which
14. how
15. that

Progressive Tense Exercises answers

1. I am watching TV.
2. I am riding my bike.
3. I am washing my hair.
4. I am eating lunch.
5. I am playing chess
6. We were sleeping when the thunderstorm started.
7. We were studying for the test because we didn't want to fail.
8. We were swimming in the deep end of the pool when the lifeguard announced the pool was closing.
9. We were reading quietly when the teacher announced a surprise quiz.
10. I was watching videos on my phone when the battery died.
11. will be playing
12. am going to be studying

13. will be watching
14. will be traveling
15. are going to be arriving

Modal Verbs Exercise answers

1. can
2. might
3. may
4. should
5. would
6. must
7. must
8. Can
9. cannot (or can't)
10. could
11. must
12. must
13. could
14. ought to
15. will

Adjective Order Exercise answers

1. d
2. a
3. b
4. c
5. d
6. c
7. c
8. a
9. b
10. a

Preposition Exercise answers

1. in
2. to
3. by
4. in
5. regarding
6. of
7. under
8. around
9. on
10. down

Find the Prepositional Phrase answers

1. before you leap –ADV
2. into things – ADV
3. across the nation – ADJ
4. in time – ADJ
5. of prevention – ADJ
6. after lunch – ADV
7. during the test period – ADV
8. between two opinions – ADV
9. except for Lawanda -- ADJ
10. off the couch – ADV

Complete Sentence Exercise answers

1. Stop right there
2. gave her grandmother a hug
3. enjoyed reading that book
4. are coming over tonight
5. think that's incorrect
6. ran a 10k
7. is 14 years old

8. revolves around the sun
9. is awesome
10. is taller than Jim

Fragment or Complete Sentence Exercise answers

1. F
2. C
3. F
4. F
5. C
6. C
7. F
8. F
9. C
10. C

Run-on Sentence Exercise answers

1. R
2. R
3. C
4. C
5. C
6. R
7. C
8. R
9. C
10. R

Homophone Exercise answers

1. principal
2. flour
3. four

4. too
5. whole
6. waste
7. it's
8. its
9. to
10. there
11. right
12. weight
13. steel
14. they're
15. two
16. stare
17. piece
18. bear
19. brake
20. son
21. hour
22. their
23. pour
24. plain
25. pair

Capitalization Exercise answers

1. NO CHANGE
2. That's Easy for You to Say!
3. Cheaper by the Dozen
4. Chicago, Illinois
5. I would like to make an appointment with Doctor Jones
6. "Be careful, Frank!" yelled Coach Johnson.
7. After the game, a reporter interviewed the coach.
8. Last year on vacation, we went to Yellowstone National Park.
9. NO CHANGE
10. Muslims believe in Allah and follow the teachings of the Koran.

11. Bill Gates was the founder of the company called Microsoft.
12. My great-grandfather fought in World War II.
13. Christmas and New Year's Day are always one week apart.
14. Dear Reverend Swanson,
15. In my opinion, no salad is complete without Italian dressing.

Commas and Quotation Marks Exercise answers

1. "Do you know what time it is?" the little girl asked.
2. "That's strange," thought Cindy, "the puppy was just here but now he's gone."
3. Mrs. Rojas said, "Please raise your hand if you're still working on the test."
4. Mom asked, "Who wants to help me with the dishes?"
5. Bonnie said, "I think that's the best field trip we've ever been on."

Coordinating Conjunctions Exercise answers

1. I'm a light sleeper, but my sister is a very deep sleeper.
2. I play soccer, and I am becoming a better player every year.
3. Do you want to play checkers, or do you want to play chess?
4. It was raining very hard, so I grabbed my umbrella.
5. We went to the zoo, and we went to the art museum.

Spelling Exercise answers

1. c
2. a
3. a
4. b
5. d
6. d
7. b
8. b
9. a

10. b

Being Concise Exercise answers

1. I arrive at school every day at 8 AM. | I arrive at school every weekday at 8 AM.
2. During the California Gold Rush
3. Joe was smiling because he passed the test.
4. If it starts raining, we'll go inside.
5. There are 50 states in America. | Currently, there are 50 states in America.

Connotation and Denotation Exercise answers

1. b
2. d
3. a
4. d
5. c
6. d
7. a
8. b
9. c
10. c

Using Punctuation for Effect Exercise answers

1. The three Rs--reading, 'riting, and 'rithmetic--form the foundation of education.
2. The big game--the one I've been telling you about all week--starts in exactly one hour.
3. As the crowd cheered him on, Rico bent his knees, swung for the fences--and struck out.
4. I can't believe I got a 100 on my math test--a 100!
5. That's the first 100 I've ever gotten on a math test--actually it's the first 100 I've ever gotten on any test.

6. My favorite author--the only one whose books I read again and again—is J.K. Rowling.

7. Four teams are left: Chicago, Dallas, New York, and Los Angeles.

8. There's only one person who can save us: Superman.

9. I only ask for one thing, class: that everyone does his or her best.

10. I had to make a decision: go to Ann's house after school, or go to Brenda's house.

11. They lost again today; that makes 20 games lost in a row.

12. It's half past five; Grandma and Grandpa should be here any minute.

13. It looks like rain; I'd better take an umbrella.

14. This is Tony's classroom; Tammy's classroom is down the hall.

15. We have to arrive at school early; we're going on a field trip.

Formal and Informal English Exercise answers

1. F
2. I
3. F
4. F
5. F
6. I
7. I
8. F
9. I
10. I

Vocabulary Exercise 1 answers

1. pupil
2. agriculture
3. fortunate
4. auditorium
5. population

6. assist
7. vertical
8. lecture
9. recognize
10. accomplish
11. curiosity
12. suggest
13. slender
14. mature
15. superb
16. seldom
17. pleasure
18. compassion
19. massive
20. admire

Vocabulary Exercise 2 answers

1. hesitate
2. annually
3. tremble
4. plead
5. biology
6. boundary
7. companion
8. thrifty
9. elevate
10. tarnish
11. circular
12. decrease
13. quench
14. foreign
15. furnish
16. request
17. coarse

18. environment
19. predict
20. absent

Greek and Latin Roots, Prefixes and Suffixes answers

1. earth
2. far
3. body
4. measure
5. heat
6. small
7. many
8. write
9. star
10. life
11. year
12. carry
13. bend
14. all
15. see
16. speech
17. sound
18. excessive
19. opposite
20. not

Similes and Metaphors Exercise answers

1. Trent turns into a bulldozer | Trent turns into a strong person who runs other players over
2. like a dream come true | it was something I had wanted to do for a long time
3. as white as a ghost | very, very pale

4. The Yankees are the 800 pound gorilla | the Yankees are a very powerful team others are afraid of
5. he's a vacuum cleaner | he eats so much it's as if he just vacuums food into his mouth
6. like a big blue blanket | the sky covers the whole world
7. Just like clockwork | the cat is as reliable as a clock
8. you're a magician in the kitchen | Mrs. Jones is an extremely good cook
9. like a giraffe | Sam was much taller than the others, so he stood out
10. You're an angel | you're a very nice person

Idioms Exercise answers

1. telling a person something that's not true but pretending that it is
2. someone who talks tough, but really isn't
3. raining extremely hard
4. go to bed
5. extremely expensive
6. got very angry
7. someone who spends a lot of time on the couch
8. going out of your way not to make someone angry or unhappy
9. wait; calm down
10. in trouble

Proverbs Exercise answers

1. the mice will play
2. home
3. before they hatch
4. louder than words
5. catches the worm
6. deserves another
7. and eat it, too
8. in one basket
9. are soon parted
10. the eye of the beholder

Antonym Exercise answers

1. hideous
2. inferior
3. rare
4. stingy
5. friendly
6. boring
7. seldom
8. temporary
9. loyalty
10. folly
11. slow
12. clumsy
13. shame
14. failure
15. liquid
16. organized
17. close
18. dislike
19. dull
20. weakness

Synonym Exercise answers

1. frailty
2. regal
3. prize
4. thing
5. leap
6. anxious
7. hilarious
8. depressed
9. shrub

10. ocean
11. total
12. cyclone
13. purchase
14. powerful
15. rock
16. foolish
17. squirm
18. city
19. intelligent
20. sleepy

Practice Test Answers

Practice Test #1

Answers and Explanations

1. A: is the best choice because paragraph 4 indicates that the story is set in spring. B, C, and D are not the best choices because the story is set in spring.

2. B: is the best choice because paragraph 16 explains that a dojo is a karate school. A, C, and D are not the best choices because they present incorrect definitions of the word "dojo".

3. D: is the best choice because the correct definition of "conferred" is "discussed." A, B, and C are not the best choices because they are not proper definitions of "conferred."

4. A: is the best choice because Joe invites Keith to the tournament so that Keith will understand that karate is important to Joe. B and D are not the best choices because they do not accurately represent Joe's attitude in the story. C is not the best choice because it does not represent Joe's main motivation for inviting Keith to the tournament.

5. Part A: B: is the best choice because Keith's attitude changes from thinking karate is boring to hoping to attend another tournament. A is not the best choice because Keith's attitude does change throughout the story. C and D are not the best choices because they do not accurately represent the change in Keith's attitude.

Part B: This sentence is from paragraph 6 and shows how Keith feels: "It sounds boring," Keith said. By paragraph 28 his attitude has changed and the story states, "Keith hoped he could attend another tournament with Joe very soon!"

6. B: is the best choice because a "green belt" properly completes the sequence. A, C, and D are not the best choices because they are not standard karate belt colors and cannot complete the presented sequence.

7. Part A: is the best choice because the primary purpose of the story is to show that karate is important to Joe. C is a good answer, but it is not the best choice because it does not reflect the primary purpose of the story. B and D are not the best choices because they do not represent themes or purposes from the story.

Part B: B: This sentence shows how committed Joe is to Karate and it shows that it is important enough to him to not skip his tournament.

8. D: is the best choice because karate is very important to Joe, so he is very likely to keep practicing it. A, B, and C are not the best choices because they do not accurately represent Joe's likelihood of continuing to practice karate.

9. Part A: C: is the best choice because it is a fact that Joe's father and grandfather both practice karate. A, B, and D are not the best choices because they are all statements of opinion instead of fact.

Part B: D: This sentence supports the fact that Joe's father and grandfather both practice karate.

10. B: is the best choice because karate is part of Joe's family heritage, as three generations of his family practice karate. A and D are good answers, but they are not the best choices because they do not demonstrate how Joe's family heritage involves karate. C is not the best choice because it does not express how karate honors Joe's family heritage.

11. A good summary of this story would read something like:

Joe invited Keith to come to his Karate tournament. At first Keith thought it would be boring and did not want to go, but once he was there he loved it. He liked learning about the sport and watching his friend compete. In the end he even decide he would like to go again.

12. C: In the story Joe says that he hopes he can reach a black belt so that he can teach karate one day.

13. C: is the best choice because the official name of the Alamo is San Antonio de Valero. A, B, and D are not the best choices because they list incorrect official names for the Alamo.

14. A: is the best choice because the author's purpose in writing "Remember the Alamo" is clearly to inform. B, C, and D are not the best choices because they represent inaccurate purposes for the story.

15. D: is the best choice because freedom was the main motivation for those who fought at the Alamo. A, B, and C are not the best choices because they do not portray the primary motivation for the Alamo fighters.

16. B: is the best choice because the Alamo was designed to serve many purposes in the community. A, C, and D are not the best choices because they do not reflect the real purpose behind the design of the Alamo.

17. D: is the best choice because it is a statement of opinion. A, B, and C are not the best choices because they are all statements of fact.

18. A: is the best choice because 184 Americans died defending the Alamo. B, C, and D are not the best choices because they are inaccurate answers.

19. II, III, IV: Jim Bowie, Davy Crockett, and General Santa Anna were all at the Battle of the Alamo. General Sam Houston fought General Santa Anna's army later, and Andrew Jackson was president at that time.

20. C: is the best choice because the story states that the Alamo is located in downtown San Antonio. A, B, and D are not the best choices because they name incorrect locations for the Alamo.

21. B: is the best choice because according to paragraph 6, the old bell is Eric's favorite artifact. A, C, and D are not the best choices because none of those things are Eric's favorite artifact.

22. C: is the best answer because it accurately completes the schedule for Eric's class trip. A, B, and D are not the best choices because they do not properly represent the events of the class trip.

23. A: is the best choice because the story says Eric was excited to see where the battle occurred. B, C, and D are not the best choices because they reflect inaccurate motivations for Eric's excitement.

24. B: is the best choice because the best definition for the word "artifacts" is "historical items". A, C, and D are not the best choices because they are incorrect definitions.

25. Part A: C: is the best choice because paragraph 6 describes Eric's favorite experiences at the Alamo. A, B, and D are not the best choices because those paragraphs do not describe Eric's favorite experiences.

Part B: A: This sentence comes from paragraph 6 and talks about one of Eric's favorite experiences.

26. D: is the best choice because the two stories both have a central theme of the history of the Alamo, linking them together. While A, B, and C are mentioned in both stories, they are not the best choices because they do not represent central themes in the stories.

27. C: is the best choice because the biggest difference between the two stories is that one is nonfiction and the other is fiction. While A, B, and D all represent differences between the stories, they are not the best choices because those differences are not as fundamental as the difference between nonfiction and fiction.

28. D: is the best choice: Uncle Eddie is qualified to teach guitar because he plays very well. A, B, and C are not the best choices because they do not represent Uncle Eddie's best qualification to teach guitar.

29. A: is the best choice because the tuning pegs of a guitar are used to help the strings make the right note. B, C, and D are not the best choices because they are not used to help tune the guitar.

30. A: is the best choice because "intently" means "in a focused way." B, C, and D are not the best choices because they do not represent accurate definitions of "intently."

31. B: is the best choice because it best completes the sequence of the story. A, C, and D are not the best choices because they do not complete the sequence according to the progression of the story.

32. D: is the best choice because the main theme of the story is to show that learning to play the guitar takes hard work. A, B, and C are not the best choices because they do not represent the main theme of the story.

33. C: is the best choice because this story is written in third person. A, B, and D are not the best choices because they represent incorrect points of view for this story.

34. A: is the best choice because Uncle Eddie feels playing the guitar will be hard, but Kari feels it will be easy. B, C, and D are not the best choices because they represent inaccurate perspectives for Uncle Eddie and Kari according to the story.

35. C: is the best choice because paragraph 14 says "Kari sighed" as the author's way of indicating Kari's displeasure. A, B, and D are not the best choices because they do not reference details included in paragraph 14.

36. B: is the best choice because Uncle Eddie is playing the "horrible music" Kari hears in paragraph 26. A, C, and D are not the best choices because they do not represent the correct person who is playing the "horrible music."

37. A: is the best choice because it is the only statement of fact from the story. B, C, and D are not the best choices because they are all statements of opinion instead of fact.

38 B: In paragraph 19, the word "bridge" is used to describe the piece of wood that holds the guitar strings.

39. There are several parts of the guitar mentioned in the story. Any four of the following are acceptable answers: body, neck, tuning pegs, strings, bridge, fingerboard, frets, and the sounding board.

40. B: In paragraph 25, Kari says "Maybe the guitar isn't for me," This sounds like she has given up.

Practice Test #2

Answers and Explanations

1. B: is the best choice because this story is set at Grandma's house. A, C, and D are not the best choices because they do not accurately represent the setting for the story.

2. A: is the best choice because the main theme of this story is that there are many different ways to have fun. B, C, and D are not the best choices because they are not main themes of the story.

3. C: is the best choice because paragraph 1 indicates that Becca thinks Grandma is "dull". A, B, and D are not the best choices because "dull" is the only word specifically used by the author to describe Becca's feelings about Grandma's house.

4. Part A: B: is the best choice because it most accurately represents the change in Becca's attitude between the beginning and end of the story. A, C, and D are not the best choices because they do not accurately describe the changes in Becca's attitude between the beginning and end of the story.

Part B: C: The point where Becca's attitude starts to change is when Grandma starts telling her about the fun things she did as a kid. Becca decides to do some of these things and she starts having fun.

5. II, III, V: In paragraph 11, Grandma talks about doing all three of these things as a kid.

6. A: is the best choice because the author's main purpose in writing this story is to entertain the reader. B, C, and D are not the best choices because the purpose of the story is not to inform, persuade, or influence.

7. C: is the best choice because it is the only statement of fact. A, B, and D are not the best choices because they are all statements of opinion.

8. B: is the best choice because the story says Becca and Grandma ate lunch in a blanket fort. A, C, and D are not the best choices because they do not accurately describe where Becca and Grandma ate lunch.

9. Part A: D: is the best choice because in paragraph 8 Becca asked Grandma to get a computer. A, B, and C are not the best choices because Becca did not ask Grandma to get a dog, TV, or car.

Part B: C: When Becca asks Grandma for a computer her response is, "We didn't have computers or game systems when I was young,"

10. B: is the best choice because Grandma has the most positive attitude in this story. A and C are not the best choices because Becca and her mom do not clearly demonstrate positive attitudes throughout this story. D is not the best choice because Grandma does have a positive attitude.

11. B: is the best choice because paragraph 22 is the first paragraph to show the change in Becca's attitude. A, C, and D are not the best choices because paragraphs 10, 24, and 26 are not the first paragraphs to show the change in Becca's attitude.

12. B: The five tribes mentioned are the Iroquois, Choctaw, Cherokee, Plains Indians, and Hopi.

13. B: is the best choice because the main purpose of dance in Native American culture is to communicate a message. A, C, and D are not the best choices because they do not accurately reflect the main purpose of dance in Native American culture.

14. A: is the best choice because the Iroquois corn husk dance and the Hopi Snake Ceremonial were both intended to bring good crops. B, C, and D are not the best choices because they do not represent the purpose of these dances.

15. I, II, IV: All of these statements can be proven as true and are not debatable.

16. C: is the best choice because in many Native American tribes the eagle feather represents strength. A, B, and D are not the best choices because they do not reflect the meaning of the eagle feather in many Native American tribes.

17. A: is the best choice because the author's main purpose in writing this article is to inform the reader. B, C, and D are not the best choices because the author's primary purpose in writing this article is not to entertain, to influence, or to persuade.

18. B: is the best choice because paragraph 1 indicates the narrator is of Cherokee heritage. A, C, and D are not the best choices because the narrator is not of Hopi, Iroquois, or Choctaw heritage.

19. A: is the best choice because this story is written in first person. B, C, and D are not the best choices because they do not accurately represent the point of view in which this story is written.

20. A: is the best choice because the main theme of this story is that Native American dancing tells a story. B, C, and D are not the best choices because they do not accurately represent the main theme of this story.

21. D: is the best choice because it is the only statement of opinion. A, B, and C are not the best choices because they are all statements of fact.

22. B: is the best choice because the story indicates the narrator was looking at the items for sale on the tables before the dancing began. A, C, and D are not the best choices because they do not accurately reflect what the narrator was doing before the dancing began.

23. A: "Pulsing" refers to the steady beating of the drum.